Breaking
the
Stress Code

Master the Art
of Calm & Control

Introduction: Taking Control of Your Inner Peace

Stress is an inevitable part of modern life, but it doesn't have to control you. Imagine waking up each day with a sense of calm and clarity, ready to tackle whatever comes your way. Picture yourself facing challenges with confidence, viewing them not as insurmountable obstacles but as opportunities to grow. This is not a distant dream—it's a reality that can be yours with the right tools and mindset.

Stress, when left unchecked, can feel overwhelming. It affects your mental, emotional, and physical well-being, influencing everything from your productivity to your relationships. However, stress doesn't have to be your enemy. With the right approach, it can become a source of strength—a catalyst for change and growth.

This book is your ultimate guide to mastering stress. It's not about eliminating stress entirely—that's neither realistic nor beneficial. Instead, it's about transforming your relationship with stress. You'll learn to understand its origins, recognize its triggers, and apply practical strategies to navigate it effectively.

Through science-backed techniques, real-life examples, and actionable exercises, this book will empower you to take control of your inner peace. Whether you're facing workplace pressures, personal struggles, or the daily grind of modern living, you'll discover tools to rise above the chaos and build a life of balance and empowerment.

By the time you finish this journey, you'll have a roadmap to a more peaceful, confident, and fulfilling life. The power to thrive under pressure is already within you—this book will show you how to unlock it. Let's begin this transformative journey together.

Table of Contents

Chapter 1: Understanding Stress

- What is Stress? The Science Behind It
- Types of Stress: Acute, Chronic, and Eustress
- The Impact of Stress on Your Mind and Body
- The Stress Cycle: How to Break Free

Takeaway: Awareness is the first step to mastery. By understanding stress, you can learn to manage it effectively.

Chapter 2: Mindset Makeover

- The Power of Positive Thinking
- Shifting from Reactivity to Proactivity
- The Role of Self-Talk in Stress Management
- Cultivating Gratitude as a Stress Reliever

Exercise: Daily Affirmations and Journaling Prompts to Build Resilience

---

Chapter 3: Time Mastery and Boundaries

- The Art of Prioritization: Focus on What Matters
- Learning to Say "No" Without Guilt
- Time Management Techniques to Reduce Overwhelm
- How to Create a Balanced Daily Routine

Tool: A customizable daily planner template for scheduling stress-free days.

Chapter 4: Breathing Life into Calm

- The Science of Breath and Stress Reduction
- Practical Breathing Exercises for Instant Calm
- Guided Meditation for Mindfulness and Relaxation

Bonus: Links to free online guided meditation resources.

Chapter 5: Physical Strategies to Combat Stress

- The Role of Exercise in Stress Management
- Nutrition Hacks to Support a Balanced Mind
- Sleep Hygiene: Restorative Practices for Better Rest
- Relaxation Techniques: Yoga, Massage, and Beyond

Case Study: How a Busy Professional Used These Tips to Reclaim Their Calm

---

Chapter 6: Building Emotional Resilience

- Identifying and Managing Triggers
- Emotional Intelligence: The Key to Inner Peace
- Letting Go of Perfectionism
- Forgiveness as a Path to Healing

Exercise: Emotional Check-In Worksheets

Chapter 7: Leveraging Support Systems

- The Importance of Community and Connection
- How to Seek and Accept Help
- Building a Personal Stress Management Toolkit

Reflection: Create Your Stress-Resilience Network

Chapter 8: Long-Term Stress Mastery

- Setting Goals for a Stress-Free Future
- Embracing a Growth Mindset
- Daily Habits for Lifelong Balance

Plan: A 30-Day Stress Mastery Challenge

Chapter 9: The Role of Technology in Stress Management

- Digital Detox: Recognizing the Stressors in Your Devices
- Mindful Tech Use: Apps and Tools That Help Instead of Harm
- Work-Life Balance in a Hyper-Connected World

Tool: A checklist for a healthy relationship with technology.

Chapter 10: The Art of Saying No Without Guilt

- Why "No" is a Complete Sentence
- Setting Boundaries in Personal and Professional Life
- Communicating Assertively Without Alienating Others

Exercise: Practice scenarios for saying no effectively.

Chapter 11: Harnessing Creativity for Stress Relief

- The Connection Between Creativity and Emotional Well-being
- Journaling, Drawing, and Music as Therapeutic Outlets
- Using Play to Reignite Joy and Reduce Tension

Activity: Guided prompts for creative expression.

Chapter 12: Financial Stress and How to Manage It

- Understanding the Sources of Financial Anxiety
- Budgeting Basics to Regain Control
- Cultivating an Abundance Mindset Despite Challenges

Tool: A financial stress assessment and action plan.

Chapter 13: Parenting and Stress: Finding the Balance

- Juggling Parenthood and Self-Care
- Teaching Stress Management to Kids
- Creating a Calm Family Environment

Activity: Stress-reducing activities for parents and children.

Chapter 14: Cultural Perspectives on Stress Management

- Stress Reduction Practices Around the World
- Incorporating Global Wisdom: Ayurveda, Tai Chi, and More
- What We Can Learn from Cultures with Lower Stress Levels

Insight: A comparison of stress management strategies across cultures.

Chapter 15: Crisis Stress Management

- Coping During Major Life Events (Loss, Divorce, Career Changes)
- Building a Crisis-Response Plan
- Finding Professional Help When You Need It

Checklist: Steps to take in a personal or professional crisis.

Conclusion: Becoming the Master of Your Inner World

Bonus Content:

- Quick Reference Cheat Sheet for Managing Stress
- Recommended Apps and Tools for Stress Management
- Exclusive Access to Online Resources and Support Groups

Chapter 1: Understanding Stress

What is Stress? The Science Behind It

Stress is a universal experience—one that transcends age, culture, and circumstance. At its core, stress is your body's way of responding to any demand or perceived threat. When you encounter a challenge, your brain activates the hypothalamus, which signals your adrenal glands to release stress hormones like cortisol and adrenaline. These hormones prepare your body for action: your heart rate increases, breathing quickens, and muscles tense. This physiological response is often referred to as the "fight-or-flight" response.

This mechanism evolved to help early humans survive immediate dangers, such as escaping predators.

However, in today's world, the same response is triggered by modern challenges—like looming deadlines, financial worries, or relationship tensions—that rarely require physical action. While short bursts of stress can be beneficial, chronic activation of this system can have profound negative effects on your health and well-being.

Stress is not inherently bad; it's how you respond to it that makes the difference. Understanding the science behind stress is the first step in transforming it into a manageable, even productive, part of your life.

Types of Stress: Acute, Chronic, and Eustress

To effectively manage stress, it's important to recognize its different forms and how they impact you.

- **Acute Stress:**
  This is the most common form of stress and is typically short-lived. It arises in response to immediate pressures, like giving a speech, navigating traffic, or handling a last-minute task. Acute stress can sharpen your focus and push you to perform better. However, frequent episodes can take a toll on your body and mind, leading to symptoms like headaches, fatigue, or irritability.
- **Chronic Stress:**
  Chronic stress is long-term and often stems from ongoing challenges, such as a toxic work environment, financial hardship, or unresolved personal conflicts. Unlike acute stress, chronic stress doesn't easily subside and can quietly wear you down over time. It increases your risk of developing serious health problems, such as hypertension, cardiovascular disease, and mental health disorders like depression and anxiety.

- **Eustress:**
  Not all stress is negative. Eustress is a positive form of stress that motivates you to grow and excel. For example, the excitement of starting a new job or the adrenaline rush before a big performance can push you to achieve your goals.

  Eustress enhances creativity, focus, and productivity, making it a valuable asset when balanced effectively.

By identifying which type of stress you're experiencing, you can adopt the right strategies to address it.

The Impact of Stress on Your Mind and Body

Stress doesn't exist in isolation—it permeates every aspect of your life, influencing your mental, physical, and emotional health. Here's how stress manifests:

- **Mental Impact:**
  Stress affects your ability to think clearly and make sound decisions. Chronic stress can impair memory, reduce concentration, and make you more prone to mental health issues like anxiety, depression, and burnout. You may find yourself feeling overwhelmed or unable to focus, which can create a vicious cycle of frustration and self-doubt.
- **Physical Impact:**
  The physical toll of stress is significant. It weakens your immune system, disrupts digestion, and can lead to headaches, fatigue, and insomnia. Prolonged stress increases the risk of chronic illnesses such as heart disease, diabetes, and gastrointestinal disorders. You might notice physical signs like muscle tension, weight fluctuations, or frequent colds and infections.

- **Behavioral Impact:**
  Stress can alter your behavior and coping mechanisms. Some people turn to unhealthy habits like overeating, smoking, or excessive alcohol consumption. Others may withdraw socially, procrastinate, or become overly irritable. Recognizing these patterns is crucial to breaking free from stress's grip.

The Stress Cycle: How to Break Free

The stress cycle begins when your brain perceives a threat, triggering a cascade of physiological and emotional responses. If left unchecked, the cycle perpetuates itself, making stress a constant presence in your life. Breaking this cycle requires intentional action and self-awareness:

1. **Recognize the Trigger:**
   Stress often begins with a specific event or thought. Identifying the source of your stress—whether it's an external factor like a demanding job or an internal one like self-criticism—is the first step to addressing it.
2. **Pause and Breathe:**
   Breathing deeply and slowly signals your body to deactivate the stress response. Techniques like diaphragmatic breathing, box breathing, or simply taking a moment to pause can help calm your nervous system.
3. **Reframe Your Perspective:**
   Shift your mindset to view stress as an opportunity for growth rather than a threat. Ask yourself, "What can I learn from this situation?" or "How can I approach this challenge differently?"
4. **Engage in Physical Activity:**
   Exercise is one of the most effective ways to break the stress cycle. Physical movement releases endorphins, improves mood, and helps your body metabolize stress hormones. Even a brisk walk can work wonders.

5. **Seek Solutions:**
   Once you've calmed your immediate stress response, tackle the root cause. Develop a plan to address the issue, whether it involves setting boundaries, seeking help, or making lifestyle changes.
6. **Adopt Long-Term Habits:**
   Incorporate regular practices like mindfulness, meditation, and healthy lifestyle choices to build resilience against future stressors.

Takeaway: Awareness is the First Step to Mastery

Stress is not something you can avoid entirely, but it is something you can manage and even harness to your advantage. By understanding the science of stress, recognizing its different types, and learning how it impacts your life, you equip yourself with the knowledge to take control. Breaking the stress cycle and adopting healthier responses will empower you to face challenges with confidence and grace.

The journey to mastering stress begins with awareness—and this is just the start. In the chapters ahead, you'll explore powerful strategies to not only manage stress but to thrive in the face of life's pressures.

Chapter 2: Mindset Makeover

Your mindset is the foundation of how you experience and respond to stress. The thoughts you cultivate, the attitudes you embrace, and the way you perceive challenges all play a significant role in your ability to manage stress effectively. This chapter will guide you through powerful strategies to shift your mindset, transforming stress from an adversary into an ally.

The Power of Positive Thinking

Your thoughts shape your reality. When faced with stress, it's easy to fall into patterns of negativity—dwelling on worst-case scenarios or focusing solely on obstacles.

Positive thinking doesn't mean ignoring life's challenges; it means approaching them with a solutions-oriented and optimistic perspective.

- **The Science of Positivity:** Research shows that positive thinking reduces stress by lowering cortisol levels, boosting immune function, and enhancing resilience. It also improves problem-solving skills and fosters better relationships.
- **Rewiring Your Brain:** Positive thinking can be cultivated through practice. Start by reframing negative thoughts into constructive ones. For instance, instead of thinking, *"I can't handle this,"* replace it with, *"I'll tackle this one step at a time."*

By consciously choosing to see possibilities rather than limitations, you'll train your mind to find calm even in chaos.

Shifting from Reactivity to Proactivity

Stress often arises when you feel out of control—reacting impulsively to situations rather than addressing them with intention. Shifting from a reactive to a proactive mindset allows you to anticipate challenges and take thoughtful action.

- **Identify Triggers:** Understanding what triggers your stress gives you the power to prepare and respond effectively. Reflect on recent stressful situations and pinpoint what set them off.

- **Pause and Respond:** When you feel overwhelmed, take a moment to pause. Practice mindfulness or deep breathing before deciding how to act. This short pause can prevent emotional reactions and encourage thoughtful responses.
- **Take Ownership:** Adopting a proactive mindset means taking responsibility for your choices and focusing on what you can control. While you can't always change circumstances, you can control your attitude and actions.

By proactively addressing stress, you empower yourself to manage it with confidence and clarity.

The Role of Self-Talk in Stress Management

Your inner dialogue—the way you talk to yourself—can either amplify stress or help you manage it. Negative self-talk, such as *"I'm not good enough"* or *"I'll never figure this out,"* fuels anxiety and self-doubt. Positive self-talk, on the other hand, encourages resilience and self-assurance.

- **Identify Negative Patterns:** Pay attention to recurring negative thoughts. Write them down to gain clarity and recognize their patterns.
- **Challenge and Reframe:** Question the validity of negative thoughts. Replace *"I always mess things up"* with *"I've overcome challenges before, and I can do it again."*
- **Speak with Kindness:** Treat yourself with the same compassion and encouragement you would offer a close friend. Practice phrases like, *"I am doing my best,"* or *"I am capable of growth and improvement."*

Self-talk isn't just about boosting confidence—it's a powerful tool for reducing stress and fostering emotional balance.

Cultivating Gratitude as a Stress Reliever

Gratitude is a simple yet transformative practice that shifts your focus from what's lacking to what you have. By regularly acknowledging your blessings, you create a buffer against stress and cultivate a more positive outlook.

- **The Benefits of Gratitude:** Studies show that gratitude improves mental health, enhances relationships, and reduces stress. It rewires your brain to focus on positivity and abundance.
- **Gratitude Practices:**
  - **Gratitude Journaling:** Each day, write down three things you're grateful for. Be specific and reflect on why they matter to you.
  - **Gratitude Rituals:** Begin or end your day by silently expressing thanks for the people, experiences, or simple joys in your life.
  - **Express Appreciation:** Take time to thank those who contribute positively to your life, whether it's a friend, colleague, or family member.

Gratitude doesn't eliminate challenges, but it equips you with a mindset to navigate them with grace.

Exercise: Daily Affirmations and Journaling Prompts to Build Resilience

To reinforce the concepts in this chapter, practice the following daily exercises:

1. **Daily Affirmations:** Start your day with positive affirmations tailored to your goals and challenges. Examples include:
   - *"I am capable of handling whatever comes my way."*
   - *"I choose to focus on solutions, not problems."*
   - *"Each day, I grow stronger and more resilient."*

Repeat these affirmations aloud or write them in a visible place as a reminder throughout your day.

2. **Journaling Prompts:** Dedicate 10–15 minutes each evening to reflect on the day using these prompts:
   o *What were three positive moments from today?*
   o *What is one thing I learned from today's challenges?*
   o *What am I grateful for right now?*

   Over time, these exercises will help rewire your mindset, making positivity, resilience, and gratitude habitual.

By adopting a positive, proactive mindset and engaging in daily practices, you'll build a mental foundation to handle stress effectively. As you master your thoughts, you'll find that life's pressures no longer feel insurmountable—they become opportunities to grow stronger and thrive. Let's continue this journey to a stress-free, empowered life in the next chapter!

Chapter 3: Time Mastery and Boundaries

Time is one of our most valuable resources, yet it often feels like there's never enough of it. The way you manage your time significantly impacts your stress levels and overall well-being. This chapter is dedicated to helping you take control of your schedule, set boundaries that protect your peace, and create a life of balance and purpose.

The Art of Prioritization: Focus on What Matters

Not everything on your to-do list deserves equal attention. Prioritization is the key to spending your time and energy on tasks that align with your goals and values.

- **The 80/20 Rule (Pareto Principle):** Recognize that 80% of your results often come from 20% of your efforts. Focus on the tasks that have the greatest impact and delegate or eliminate less critical ones.
- **Urgent vs. Important:** Use the Eisenhower Matrix to categorize tasks into four quadrants:
    - **Urgent and Important:** Do these immediately.
    - **Important but Not Urgent:** Schedule these for later.
    - **Urgent but Not Important:** Delegate these to someone else.
    - **Neither Urgent nor Important:** Eliminate these entirely.
- **Clarify Your Goals:** Align your daily tasks with your long-term objectives. Ask yourself, *"Does this bring me closer to my goals or align with my values?"*

By focusing on what truly matters, you free yourself from unnecessary stress and create more meaningful progress.

Learning to Say "No" Without Guilt

One of the biggest time traps is the inability to say "no." Overcommitting can lead to overwhelm, resentment, and burnout. Learning to set boundaries is an essential skill for protecting your time and energy.

- **Why Saying No is Empowering:** Saying "no" allows you to focus on your priorities and prevents you from spreading yourself too thin. It's not about rejecting others—it's about honoring your own needs.

- **How to Say No Gracefully:**
  - **Be Direct but Polite:** Use clear, respectful language, such as, *"I appreciate the offer, but I won't be able to take this on right now."*
  - **Offer Alternatives:** If appropriate, suggest another resource or person who can help.
  - **Don't Over-Explain:** A simple, *"I'm not available for this,"* is enough. Avoid justifying your decision excessively.
- **Practice Makes Perfect:** Start with small "no's" and gradually work up to bigger commitments. Over time, it will feel less intimidating.

By mastering the art of saying "no," you'll reclaim valuable time and energy for the things that truly matter.

Time Management Techniques to Reduce Overwhelm

Effective time management is about working smarter, not harder. Implementing these techniques can help you reduce overwhelm and maintain control over your schedule:

- **Batch Similar Tasks:** Group similar tasks (e.g., responding to emails or making phone calls) to save mental energy and minimize switching between activities.
- **Use the Two-Minute Rule:** If a task takes less than two minutes, do it immediately rather than adding it to your to-do list.
- **Set Time Blocks:** Allocate specific time slots for focused work, breaks, and personal activities. This creates structure and prevents procrastination.
- **The Pomodoro Technique:** Work in focused intervals (e.g., 25 minutes) followed by short breaks. This method boosts productivity and helps maintain focus.
- **Review and Reflect:** Spend a few minutes at the end of each day reviewing what you accomplished and planning for tomorrow.

These techniques help you approach your time with intention, reducing the chaos that leads to stress.

How to Create a Balanced Daily Routine

A balanced routine is the cornerstone of a stress-free life. It ensures that your physical, emotional, and mental needs are met while keeping your priorities in check.

- **Morning Rituals:** Start your day with activities that energize and inspire you, such as meditation, exercise, or journaling.
- **Work-Life Balance:** Set clear boundaries between work and personal time. Avoid letting work tasks spill into your evenings or weekends.
- **Scheduled Breaks:** Incorporate short breaks throughout your day to recharge. Stepping away from tasks helps prevent burnout and maintains productivity.
- **Evening Wind-Down:** End your day with calming activities, like reading, stretching, or gratitude journaling, to prepare for restful sleep.
- **Flexibility is Key:** Life is unpredictable, so allow room for adjustments. A balanced routine is not about rigidity—it's about flow.

With a well-rounded routine, you'll create a sustainable rhythm that supports your goals and reduces stress.

Tool: A Customizable Daily Planner Template

To help you master your time, here's a customizable daily planner template. Use it to structure your day with intention and minimize overwhelm:

Daily Planner Template

Morning (Focus & Preparation):

- Gratitude: Write one thing you're thankful for today.
- Priority 1: _____
- Priority 2: _____
- Self-Care Activity: _____

Midday (Work & Productivity):

- Time Block 1: _____
- Time Block 2: _____
- Break (Activity): _____

Afternoon (Reflection & Reset):

- Priority Task: _____
- Delegated Task: _____
- Quick Wins (2-Minute Tasks): _____

Evening (Relax & Recharge):

- Reflection: What went well today?
- Gratitude: One positive moment from the day.
- Self-Care Activity: _____

By using this template and applying the techniques in this chapter, you'll create a daily framework that aligns with your priorities, protects your peace, and fosters balance.

Mastering your time and setting boundaries is a game-changer for stress management. With these tools and strategies, you'll not only reduce overwhelm but also build a life that feels purposeful and in control. In the next chapter, we'll explore breathing techniques and relaxation methods to enhance your calm even further. Let's keep building your stress-free, empowered life!

Chapter 4: Breathing Life into Calm

Your breath is one of the most powerful tools for managing stress.
It's always with you, accessible in any situation, and directly
connected to your nervous system. By learning to control your breath,
you can instantly calm your mind, relax your body, and take charge
of stressful moments. In this chapter, we'll explore the science of
breath, practical exercises, and meditative techniques to help you find
calm no matter what life throws your way.

The Science of Breath and Stress Reduction

Breathing is an automatic process controlled by the autonomic nervous system, but it's also one of the few bodily functions you can consciously control. This unique connection makes breath a powerful tool for stress management.

- **The Nervous System Connection:**
  Your breath directly impacts your autonomic nervous system, which has two branches:
    - **Sympathetic Nervous System (Fight-or-Flight):** Activated during stress, increasing heart rate, breathing, and tension.
    - **Parasympathetic Nervous System (Rest-and-Digest):** Activated during relaxation, slowing heart rate, reducing breathing, and promoting calm.

  By consciously slowing and deepening your breath, you shift from a stress response to a relaxation response, calming both your mind and body.

- **The Role of Oxygen:**
  Shallow, rapid breathing limits oxygen flow to your brain and body, exacerbating stress and anxiety. Deep breathing increases oxygen levels, improving focus, mood, and energy.

Understanding the science of breath gives you a practical, evidence-based approach to reducing stress anytime, anywhere.

Practical Breathing Exercises for Instant Calm

These simple yet effective techniques can be used in moments of stress to quickly bring calm and clarity:

1. **Diaphragmatic Breathing (Belly Breathing):**
    o Sit or lie down in a comfortable position.
    o Place one hand on your chest and the other on your belly.
    o Inhale deeply through your nose, allowing your belly to rise while keeping your chest still.
    o Exhale slowly through your mouth, letting your belly fall.
    o Repeat for 5–10 minutes.

   Benefits: Reduces tension, lowers cortisol levels, and promotes relaxation.

2. **Box Breathing:**
    o Inhale through your nose for 4 counts.
    o Hold your breath for 4 counts.
    o Exhale through your mouth for 4 counts.
    o Hold your breath again for 4 counts.
    o Repeat for several cycles.

   Benefits: Helps regulate your breath, calm your mind, and regain control during high-stress moments.

3. **Alternate Nostril Breathing (Nadi Shodhana):**
    o Sit comfortably and close your right nostril with your thumb.
    o Inhale deeply through your left nostril.
    o Close your left nostril with your ring finger, release your right nostril, and exhale through it.
    o Inhale through your right nostril, close it, and exhale through your left.
    o Continue alternating for 5–10 minutes.

   Benefits: Balances the nervous system, clears the mind, and enhances focus.

4. **4-7-8 Breathing:**
   - Inhale deeply through your nose for 4 counts.
   - Hold your breath for 7 counts.
   - Exhale slowly through your mouth for 8 counts.
   - Repeat for 4–5 cycles.

   Benefits: Quickly reduces anxiety, promotes sleep, and calms the mind.

Guided Meditation for Mindfulness and Relaxation

Breathing is the foundation of mindfulness meditation, a practice that helps you focus on the present moment and let go of stress. Here's a simple guided meditation to try:

- **Set the Scene:** Find a quiet space and sit comfortably with your back straight. Close your eyes or soften your gaze.
- **Focus on Your Breath:** Bring your attention to your breath. Notice the sensation of air entering and leaving your nostrils. Feel your chest and belly rise and fall with each breath.
- **Anchor Your Thoughts:** When your mind begins to wander (and it will), gently bring your focus back to your breath without judgment.
- **Expand Your Awareness:** After a few minutes, expand your focus to include sounds around you, sensations in your body, or the feeling of the chair beneath you.
- **End with Gratitude:** Before you open your eyes, take a moment to express gratitude for the time you've taken to care for yourself.

Suggested Duration: Start with 5 minutes and gradually increase to 15–20 minutes as you become more comfortable with the practice.

Bonus: Links to Free Online Guided Meditation Resources

For additional support in practicing mindfulness and relaxation, explore these free guided meditation resources:

1. **Insight Timer (App and Website):** Offers thousands of free guided meditations for relaxation, stress relief, and sleep.
   o Website: www.insighttimer.com
2. **Calm (App and Website):** Includes free guided meditations for beginners and advanced practitioners.
   o Website: www.calm.com
3. **The Honest Guys (YouTube Channel):** A popular source of guided meditations, relaxation music, and visualization exercises.
   o Channel: The Honest Guys on YouTube
4. **UCLA Mindful Awareness Research Center:** Provides free downloadable guided meditations for various needs.
   o Website: UCLA Mindfulness
5. **Headspace (App):** Offers free trials and free content, including short meditations for stress relief.
   o Website: www.headspace.com

Breath is a bridge between your mind and body—a tool that can calm the storm of stress and bring you back to balance. By practicing these breathing techniques and exploring guided meditations, you'll build a powerful habit that keeps you grounded and resilient in the face of life's pressures. In the next chapter, we'll explore how physical strategies like exercise and sleep can further enhance your stress management toolkit. Let's continue building your empowered, stress-free life!

Chapter 5: Physical Strategies to Combat Stress

Stress doesn't just affect your mind—it impacts your entire body. To combat it effectively, you need to engage your physical self in the process. This chapter explores how exercise, nutrition, sleep, and relaxation techniques can work together to reduce stress and restore balance to your life.

The Role of Exercise in Stress Management

Exercise is one of the most powerful natural remedies for stress. It reduces stress hormones like cortisol and releases endorphins, which are chemicals in your brain that elevate mood and create a sense of well-being.

- **Types of Exercise for Stress Relief:**
  - **Cardio Workouts:** Activities like running, cycling, or swimming increase your heart rate, helping you release built-up tension.
  - **Strength Training:** Lifting weights or doing resistance exercises improves focus and channels nervous energy.
  - **Mind-Body Exercises:** Practices like yoga, tai chi, and Pilates combine movement with mindfulness, offering a holistic approach to stress relief.
- **Making it a Habit:**
  - Start small: Aim for 20–30 minutes of moderate activity most days of the week.
  - Find what you enjoy: Choose activities you look forward to, whether it's dancing, hiking, or gardening.
  - Make it social: Exercising with friends or joining a class can add a fun and supportive element to your routine.

Quick Tip: Even a 10-minute walk can significantly lower stress and improve your mood.

Nutrition Hacks to Support a Balanced Mind

What you eat has a direct impact on how you feel. Certain foods can increase stress, while others help your body cope better with it.

- **Foods That Fight Stress:**
  - o **Omega-3 Fatty Acids:** Found in salmon, walnuts, and flaxseeds, these fats reduce inflammation and support brain health.
  - o **Complex Carbohydrates:** Whole grains, fruits, and vegetables stabilize blood sugar levels, preventing mood swings.
  - o **Magnesium-Rich Foods:** Leafy greens, nuts, and seeds help regulate stress responses and improve sleep.
  - o **Probiotic Foods:** Yogurt, kimchi, and sauerkraut promote gut health, which is closely linked to emotional well-being.
- **Foods to Limit:**
  - o **Caffeine:** Excess caffeine can increase anxiety and disrupt sleep.
  - o **Sugar:** High sugar intake causes energy crashes and mood fluctuations.
  - o **Alcohol:** While it may seem relaxing initially, alcohol can interfere with sleep and exacerbate stress over time.

Quick Snack Ideas for Stress Relief:

- A handful of mixed nuts with dark chocolate.
- Greek yogurt with fresh berries.
- Sliced avocado on whole-grain toast.

Sleep Hygiene: Restorative Practices for Better Rest

Sleep is essential for recovering from stress, but stress often disrupts sleep. Establishing good sleep hygiene practices can help you achieve deeper, more restorative rest.

- **Tips for Better Sleep:**
  - **Create a Bedtime Routine:** Develop a calming pre-sleep ritual, such as reading, meditating, or taking a warm bath.
  - **Stick to a Schedule:** Go to bed and wake up at the same time every day, even on weekends.
  - **Optimize Your Environment:** Keep your bedroom cool, dark, and quiet. Consider blackout curtains and white noise machines.
  - **Limit Screen Time:** Avoid screens for at least an hour before bed. The blue light from devices can interfere with melatonin production.
  - **Watch Your Diet:** Avoid heavy meals, caffeine, and alcohol in the evening.
- **When Sleep Problems Persist:** If stress-related insomnia continues, consider consulting a healthcare professional for support.

Relaxation Techniques: Yoga, Massage, and Beyond

Relaxation techniques help reduce tension, lower blood pressure, and promote a state of calm. Incorporating these practices into your routine can provide lasting stress relief.

- **Yoga:**
  Yoga combines movement, breath, and mindfulness to calm the mind and stretch the body. Poses like Child's Pose, Downward Dog, and Corpse Pose are particularly relaxing.
- **Massage Therapy:**
  Regular massages reduce muscle tension, improve circulation, and lower cortisol levels. Even self-massage techniques can provide relief.
- **Progressive Muscle Relaxation (PMR):**
  PMR involves tensing and then relaxing each muscle group in your body, promoting a deep sense of relaxation.

- **Hot Baths and Aromatherapy:**
  A warm bath with Epsom salts and essential oils like lavender or eucalyptus can soothe your body and mind after a long day.

Case Study: How a Busy Professional Used These Tips to Reclaim Their Calm

Meet Sarah: A marketing manager juggling a demanding career, two young children, and a busy household. Sarah often felt overwhelmed, exhausted, and disconnected. Here's how she transformed her life using the strategies in this chapter:

1. **Exercise as a Non-Negotiable:**
   Sarah started with short, 20-minute morning walks three times a week. She gradually added yoga sessions on weekends, which became a favorite way to relax and reset.
2. **Nourishing Her Body:**
   By swapping processed snacks for whole foods like nuts, fruits, and smoothies, Sarah noticed a steady improvement in her energy levels and mood.
3. **Prioritizing Sleep:**
   Sarah established a bedtime routine that included reading and a cup of chamomile tea. She began using blackout curtains, which significantly improved her sleep quality.
4. **Embracing Relaxation Techniques:**
   Once a month, Sarah treated herself to a massage. On busier weeks, she practiced progressive muscle relaxation at home, which helped her release tension and sleep better.

The Result: Within three months, Sarah felt more energized, focused, and in control. Her stress levels decreased, and she found greater joy in both her work and family life.

Physical self-care is a cornerstone of stress management. By integrating these strategies into your daily life, you'll not only reduce stress but also enhance your overall health and resilience. In the next chapter, we'll dive into emotional resilience and how to build a stronger, more adaptable mindset. Let's continue this empowering journey together!

Chapter 6: Building Emotional Resilience

Emotional resilience is your ability to bounce back from life's challenges, adapt to adversity, and thrive under pressure. While stress often tests your emotional limits, cultivating resilience empowers you to handle difficult situations with strength and grace. In this chapter, we'll explore practical strategies to identify and manage emotional triggers, develop emotional intelligence, and foster healing through self-compassion and forgiveness.

Identifying and Managing Triggers

Stress often arises when certain people, situations, or memories evoke strong emotional responses. Identifying these triggers is the first step to managing them effectively.

- **What Are Triggers?**
  Triggers are external or internal stimuli that provoke a reaction, such as anger, frustration, or anxiety. They may include criticism, conflict, or reminders of past events.
- **How to Identify Your Triggers:**
  - **Keep a Journal:** Record moments of intense emotional reactions. Note what happened, how you felt, and what thoughts arose.
  - **Look for Patterns:** Over time, patterns will emerge, helping you pinpoint specific triggers.
  - **Evaluate Underlying Beliefs:** Sometimes, triggers stem from limiting beliefs or unresolved issues, such as fear of failure or rejection.
- **Managing Triggers:**
  - **Pause and Reflect:** When triggered, take a moment to pause and breathe before reacting.
  - **Set Boundaries:** Limit exposure to triggering situations or individuals when possible.
  - **Reframe Your Perspective:** View triggers as opportunities for growth rather than threats to your well-being.

Emotional Intelligence: The Key to Inner Peace

Emotional intelligence (EI) is your ability to understand, manage, and express your emotions while empathizing with others. Developing EI helps you navigate stressful situations with calm and clarity.

- **The Four Pillars of Emotional Intelligence:**
  1. **Self-Awareness:** Recognize your emotions and their impact on your thoughts and behavior.
  2. **Self-Regulation:** Control impulsive reactions and adapt to changing circumstances.
  3. **Empathy:** Understand and share the feelings of others.
  4. **Social Skills:** Build healthy relationships and communicate effectively.
- **How to Improve EI:**
  - **Practice Mindfulness:** Observe your emotions without judgment.
  - **Ask Questions:** When feeling overwhelmed, ask, *"Why am I reacting this way?"*
  - **Seek Feedback:** Trusted friends or mentors can provide insights into how your emotions affect others.
  - **Develop Empathy:** Practice active listening and put yourself in others' shoes.

Emotional intelligence allows you to respond to stress with composure and cultivate meaningful connections, both of which enhance resilience.

Letting Go of Perfectionism

Perfectionism can be a significant source of stress, creating unrealistic expectations and fostering feelings of inadequacy when goals aren't met. Letting go of perfectionism frees you to embrace progress over perfection.

- **The Problem with Perfectionism:**
  - **Unrealistic Standards:** Setting impossible goals leads to frustration and burnout.
  - **Fear of Failure:** Perfectionism often stems from a fear of making mistakes or being judged.
  - **Procrastination:** The pressure to be perfect can cause delays in starting or finishing tasks.

- **How to Overcome Perfectionism:**
  - **Embrace the Growth Mindset:** View mistakes as opportunities to learn and grow.
  - **Set Realistic Goals:** Break tasks into achievable steps and celebrate small wins.
  - **Practice Self-Compassion:** Speak to yourself with kindness and encouragement, especially when things don't go as planned.
  - **Redefine Success:** Focus on effort and improvement rather than flawless results.

By releasing the need for perfection, you'll experience less stress and more joy in both your achievements and your journey.

Forgiveness as a Path to Healing

Holding onto resentment or guilt can weigh heavily on your emotional well-being. Forgiveness—whether directed toward others or yourself—is a powerful act of liberation.

- **The Benefits of Forgiveness:**
  - **Emotional Freedom:** Letting go of grudges reduces anger and bitterness.
  - **Improved Relationships:** Forgiveness fosters understanding and empathy.
  - **Physical Health:** Studies show that forgiveness can lower blood pressure and improve immune function.
- **How to Forgive:**
  - **Acknowledge Your Feelings:** Allow yourself to feel and process anger or hurt.
  - **Shift Your Perspective:** Recognize that everyone makes mistakes and that holding onto pain only prolongs your suffering.
  - **Practice Self-Forgiveness:** Let go of guilt and remind yourself that you're human. Focus on what you've learned and how you've grown.

- o **Seek Closure:** Write a letter (even if you don't send it) to express your thoughts and release your emotions.

Forgiveness doesn't mean condoning harmful actions—it means freeing yourself from their hold on your life.

Exercise: Emotional Check-In Worksheets

Regular emotional check-ins help you build awareness, manage triggers, and maintain resilience. Use the following prompts to reflect and reset:

1. **Identify Your Emotions:**
   - o What am I feeling right now? (e.g., angry, sad, anxious, content)
   - o What triggered this emotion?
2. **Assess Your Needs:**
   - o What do I need at this moment to feel supported or grounded?
   - o Who can I turn to for help or understanding?
3. **Reframe Your Thoughts:**
   - o Is my current perspective constructive or destructive?
   - o How can I view this situation in a way that empowers me?
4. **Plan an Action Step:**
   - o What small action can I take right now to improve how I feel?
   - o How can I prepare for similar challenges in the future?

Optional: Create a habit of checking in with yourself daily, either in the morning to set intentions or in the evening to reflect on your day.

Building emotional resilience is a lifelong journey, but the rewards are transformative. By identifying your triggers, cultivating emotional intelligence, and letting go of perfectionism and resentment, you'll become stronger, more adaptable, and at peace with yourself.

In the next chapter, we'll explore how to harness support systems to further strengthen your stress management journey. Let's continue building your empowered life together!

Chapter 7: Leveraging Support Systems

Stress is easier to manage when you don't face it alone. Human connection is a fundamental need, and building a reliable support system can be a powerful tool for resilience. Whether it's family, friends, colleagues, or professional networks, the people in your life play an essential role in helping you navigate challenges. In this chapter, you'll learn how to build and lean on your support systems to reduce stress and foster a sense of belonging.

The Importance of Community and Connection

Social connections are not just nice to have—they're vital for your well-being. Strong relationships can reduce stress, provide emotional support, and even improve your physical health.

- **The Science of Connection:**
  Studies show that people with strong social ties have lower levels of stress and a reduced risk of mental health disorders. Connection releases oxytocin, a hormone that lowers cortisol and promotes feelings of trust and security.
- **Benefits of a Supportive Community:**
  - **Emotional Support:** Loved ones offer comfort and encouragement during tough times.
  - **Shared Wisdom:** A community provides diverse perspectives and advice for problem-solving.
  - **Accountability:** Support systems help you stay motivated and focused on your goals.
- **Types of Communities to Cultivate:**
  - **Personal:** Family, friends, and close relationships.
  - **Professional:** Colleagues, mentors, and industry networks.
  - **Interest-Based:** Groups centered around hobbies, causes, or shared passions.

A strong sense of connection fosters resilience and reminds you that you're never truly alone.

How to Seek and Accept Help

Asking for help can feel vulnerable, but it's an essential part of managing stress. No one is expected to handle everything alone, and reaching out shows strength, not weakness.

- **When to Seek Help:**
  - When stress feels overwhelming or unmanageable.
  - When you lack the resources or expertise to address a challenge.
  - When emotional or physical symptoms of stress persist despite your efforts.
- **How to Ask for Help:**
  - **Be Clear and Specific:** Identify what you need and communicate it directly. For example, instead of saying, *"I'm overwhelmed,"* try, *"I need help organizing this project."*
  - **Choose the Right Person:** Seek support from someone who is trustworthy and capable of helping in the specific area you're struggling with.
  - **Express Gratitude:** Acknowledge the support you receive and show appreciation for their time and effort.
- **Overcoming Barriers to Asking for Help:**
  - **Challenge Stigma:** Remind yourself that everyone needs help sometimes—it's a natural part of life.
  - **Release Guilt:** Helping others brings people joy and fulfillment, so don't feel guilty about asking.
  - **Be Open to Receiving:** Practice accepting help without minimizing or deflecting it.

By seeking and accepting support, you strengthen your resilience and build deeper connections with those around you.

Building a Personal Stress Management Toolkit

A support system is only part of the solution. Having a personal toolkit of stress-relief strategies empowers you to manage stress independently while knowing when to reach out for help.

- **Core Components of a Toolkit:**
  - **Relaxation Practices:** Breathing exercises, meditation, and progressive muscle relaxation.

- o **Physical Activities:** Walking, yoga, or any exercise that helps you release tension.
- o **Creative Outlets:** Journaling, drawing, or other forms of self-expression.
- o **Go-To Resources:** Books, podcasts, or apps that offer guidance and inspiration.
- o **Emergency Contacts:** A list of people you can turn to in times of immediate need, such as a trusted friend, therapist, or crisis hotline.
- **Customizing Your Toolkit:**
  - o Assess your stress triggers and identify what strategies work best for you.
  - o Experiment with new tools and refine your approach over time.
  - o Keep your toolkit accessible, whether it's a physical box, a journal, or a folder on your phone.

Having a personalized stress management toolkit ensures you're prepared to handle stress proactively and effectively.

Reflection: Create Your Stress-Resilience Network

Take a moment to reflect on the people and resources in your life that can form your support network. Use the following prompts to guide you:

1. **Identify Key Supporters:**
   - o Who are the people in my life I can turn to for emotional support?
   - o Who can offer practical help or advice when needed?
   - o Are there any professional resources I should consider adding, such as a therapist or coach?
2. **Assess the Strength of Your Connections:**
   - o Do I feel comfortable reaching out to these individuals?
   - o Are there relationships I need to nurture or repair?
   - o How can I show appreciation for the support I receive?

3. **Expand Your Network:**
   - ○ Are there new communities or groups I'd like to join?
   - ○ What steps can I take to connect with people who share my interests or values?
   - ○ How can I contribute to others' lives, building mutual support?
4. **Integrate Your Toolkit:**
   - ○ What strategies from my stress management toolkit complement my support network?
   - ○ How can I combine self-reliance with reaching out for help when needed?

Write down your reflections and create a visual map of your stress-resilience network. Include the people, tools, and practices that support your well-being.

Leveraging support systems is a vital part of managing stress and building resilience. By fostering strong connections, asking for help when needed, and developing a personalized toolkit, you create a safety net that empowers you to thrive. In the next chapter, we'll explore long-term strategies for mastering stress and building a balanced, fulfilling life. Let's keep moving forward on this transformative journey!

Chapter 8: Long-Term Stress Mastery

Mastering stress is not just about responding to it in the moment; it's about creating a life where stress no longer dominates. This requires adopting sustainable habits, cultivating a mindset that thrives on growth, and setting intentional goals for a balanced and fulfilling future. In this chapter, we'll explore strategies for building long-term resilience and introduce a 30-day challenge to help you solidify these practices.

Setting Goals for a Stress-Free Future

Long-term stress mastery starts with envisioning the life you want and creating actionable goals to achieve it. Goals provide direction, purpose, and a sense of control, all of which reduce stress.

- **Define Your Vision:**
    - Imagine what a stress-free life looks like for you. Consider your ideal balance between work, relationships, health, and personal growth.
    - Ask yourself, *"What areas of my life are causing the most stress, and what would I like to change?"*
- **Set SMART Goals:**
    - **Specific:** Clearly define what you want to achieve. (*Example: Meditate for 10 minutes daily.*)
    - **Measurable:** Track your progress. (*Example: Use a habit tracker to monitor your meditation practice.*)
    - **Achievable:** Set realistic goals that align with your current capacity. (*Example: Start with short meditation sessions and increase gradually.*)
    - **Relevant:** Ensure your goals align with your values and priorities.
    - **Time-Bound:** Set deadlines to keep yourself accountable. (*Example: Build a consistent meditation habit within 30 days.*)
- **Break It Down:**
    - Divide larger goals into smaller, manageable steps to prevent overwhelm.
    - Celebrate milestones to stay motivated along the way.

By setting intentional goals, you take control of your future and create a roadmap to lasting peace and balance.

Embracing a Growth Mindset

Your mindset determines how you approach challenges and stressors. A growth mindset—the belief that you can learn, grow, and improve—empowers you to view stress as an opportunity for development rather than a threat.

- **Key Principles of a Growth Mindset:**
    - **Challenges Are Opportunities:** Every stressful situation holds a lesson or chance to grow.
    - **Effort Leads to Improvement:** Persistence and hard work are more important than innate talent.
    - **Feedback Is Valuable:** Criticism and setbacks provide insights for growth.
    - **Failure Is Not Final:** Mistakes are stepping stones to success.
- **Cultivating a Growth Mindset:**
    - **Reframe Stress:** Instead of thinking, *"This is too hard,"* try, *"This is a chance to learn and grow."*
    - **Practice Self-Compassion:** Treat yourself with kindness during difficult times, recognizing that growth takes time.
    - **Seek Learning Opportunities:** Continuously develop skills and knowledge to strengthen your resilience.

A growth mindset shifts your perspective, making stress a catalyst for positive change rather than an obstacle.

Daily Habits for Lifelong Balance

Long-term stress mastery relies on consistent habits that support your physical, emotional, and mental well-being. These daily practices create a foundation of balance and resilience.

- **Morning Rituals:**
  - Start your day with activities that energize and center you, such as mindfulness, stretching, or journaling.
  - Set daily intentions to focus on what matters most.
- **Midday Resets:**
  - Incorporate short breaks to recharge, such as a walk, breathing exercises, or a quick gratitude check.
  - Stay hydrated and nourish your body with healthy snacks.
- **Evening Wind-Down:**
  - Unwind with calming activities like reading, meditation, or a warm bath.
  - Reflect on the day's successes and lessons, practicing gratitude for positive moments.
- **Weekly Practices:**
  - Schedule self-care activities, such as exercise, hobbies, or social time with loved ones.
  - Review your goals and progress, adjusting as needed.

By integrating these habits into your routine, you'll build a life that naturally resists stress and promotes balance.

Plan: A 30-Day Stress Mastery Challenge

To help you implement the strategies in this book, take on the 30-Day Stress Mastery Challenge. Each day introduces a small, actionable step to build your resilience and reduce stress. Here's the plan:

Week 1: Laying the Foundation

- Day 1: Write down your top three stressors and one goal for each.
- Day 2: Practice deep breathing for 5 minutes.
- Day 3: Start a gratitude journal and list three things you're grateful for.
- Day 4: Identify one unnecessary task to eliminate from your schedule.

- Day 5: Take a 10-minute walk outdoors.
- Day 6: Set a timer and focus on a single task for 20 minutes (Pomodoro Technique).
- Day 7: Reflect on your first week and adjust your goals if needed.

Week 2: Strengthening Your Mindset

- Day 8: Reframe a stressful situation as a learning opportunity.
- Day 9: Write a positive affirmation and repeat it throughout the day.
- Day 10: Reach out to a friend or loved one for a meaningful conversation.
- Day 11: Declutter a small space in your home or workspace.
- Day 12: Try a new relaxation technique, such as progressive muscle relaxation.
- Day 13: Commit to saying "no" to one non-essential request.
- Day 14: Reflect on your progress and celebrate a small win.

Week 3: Building Resilience

- Day 15: Start a 5-minute mindfulness meditation practice.
- Day 16: Identify one trigger and plan a healthy response.
- Day 17: Schedule a self-care activity (e.g., massage, yoga, or a favorite hobby).
- Day 18: Cook a meal with stress-relieving ingredients.
- Day 19: Practice forgiveness by writing a letter (even if you don't send it).
- Day 20: Spend 15 minutes on a creative activity, like drawing or journaling.
- Day 21: Reflect on your growth and identify areas for continued improvement.

Week 4: Sustaining Balance

- Day 22: Create a morning ritual that energizes and inspires you.
- Day 23: Write down your top three priorities for the week ahead.

- Day 24: Share a gratitude message with someone in your life.
- Day 25: Take a digital detox for at least an hour.
- Day 26: Schedule time for a hobby or passion project.
- Day 27: Use guided meditation for deep relaxation.
- Day 28: Reflect on how you've changed over the past month.

Final Days: Mastering Your Calm

- Day 29: Write a letter to your future self about your journey.
- Day 30: Celebrate your achievements and plan your next steps for lifelong stress mastery.

By setting goals, cultivating a growth mindset, and embracing daily habits, you can achieve long-term mastery over stress. This journey is a process of continuous growth, and the 30-Day Stress Mastery Challenge is just the beginning. Let's move forward with confidence and continue creating a life of balance, resilience, and empowerment!

Chapter 9: The Role of Technology in Stress Management

Technology has transformed our lives in countless positive ways, but it's also introduced new challenges that can contribute to stress. From the constant barrage of notifications to the pressure of staying connected 24/7, the digital age can feel overwhelming. However, technology doesn't have to be your enemy—it can also be a powerful ally in stress management when used mindfully. This chapter explores how to recognize digital stressors, adopt healthier tech habits, and use technology to enhance, rather than hinder, your well-being.

Digital Detox: Recognizing the Stressors in Your Devices

Our devices are designed to keep us engaged, but that constant connection can lead to feelings of overwhelm and burnout.

- **Common Tech-Related Stressors:**
    - **Notifications Overload:** Constant pings and alerts fragment your attention and increase anxiety.
    - **Social Media Comparison:** Scrolling through curated highlights of others' lives can lead to feelings of inadequacy.
    - **Always-On Work Culture:** Emails and messages outside work hours blur the boundaries between personal and professional life.
    - **Screen Time Fatigue:** Prolonged screen use can lead to eye strain, headaches, and mental exhaustion.
- **Signs You Need a Digital Detox:**
    - You feel anxious or restless without your device.
    - You lose track of time while scrolling or gaming.
    - Your sleep is disrupted by late-night screen use.
    - You struggle to focus on tasks without checking your phone.

A digital detox doesn't mean giving up technology completely—it's about creating intentional breaks to reset your relationship with your devices.

Mindful Tech Use: Apps and Tools That Help Instead of Harm

When used purposefully, technology can support your stress management efforts. The key is to use tools that enhance mindfulness, productivity, and relaxation.

- **Apps for Mindfulness and Relaxation:**
    - **Calm:** Guided meditations, breathing exercises, and sleep stories for stress relief.

- o **Headspace:** Mindfulness programs for beginners and advanced users alike.
- o **Insight Timer:** Free meditations, yoga classes, and relaxation music.
- **Apps for Productivity and Focus:**
  - o **Forest:** Grow virtual trees by staying off your phone during focus sessions.
  - o **Todoist:** A simple app to organize tasks and reduce mental clutter.
  - o **RescueTime:** Track and analyze your screen time to identify areas for improvement.
- **Apps for Better Sleep:**
  - o **Sleep Cycle:** Tracks your sleep patterns and wakes you during the lightest sleep phase.
  - o **White Noise:** Provides soothing sounds to help you relax and fall asleep faster.
- **Customizing Your Device Settings:**
  - o Use "Do Not Disturb" mode during work or relaxation periods.
  - o Turn off non-essential notifications.
  - o Enable screen time limits for apps that consume too much of your attention.

By choosing technology intentionally, you can make it work for you, not against you.

Work-Life Balance in a Hyper-Connected World

The boundaries between work and personal life have become increasingly blurred in the digital age, contributing to heightened stress levels. Establishing clear boundaries is essential for maintaining balance and protecting your well-being.

- **Strategies for Maintaining Work-Life Balance:**
  - o **Set Office Hours:** Define clear start and end times for your workday and stick to them.

- Turn Off Work Notifications After Hours: Use email scheduling tools and communicate your availability to colleagues.
  - Create a Separate Workspace: If working from home, designate a specific area for work to mentally separate it from personal life.
  - Take Regular Breaks: Step away from screens during the day to refresh your mind and prevent burnout.
  - Unplug During Personal Time: Commit to device-free meals, family time, or evenings to fully engage with loved ones.
- **The Power of Downtime:**
  - Use your free time to engage in non-digital activities, such as reading, exercising, or pursuing hobbies.
  - Prioritize quality time with friends and family, free from the distractions of screens.

Balancing technology and personal time ensures you stay productive without sacrificing your mental health.

Tool: A Checklist for a Healthy Relationship with Technology

Use this checklist to evaluate and improve your relationship with technology:

1. **Reduce Digital Clutter:**
   - Unsubscribe from unnecessary emails and newsletters.
   - Delete unused apps and files from your devices.
2. **Set Boundaries:**
   - Schedule device-free hours or "digital detox" days.
   - Turn off notifications for non-essential apps.
3. **Practice Mindful Tech Use:**
   - Ask yourself, *"Is this activity productive or relaxing?"* before engaging with your device.
   - Use apps intentionally rather than mindlessly scrolling.

4. **Optimize Your Devices:**
   - o Use blue light filters or night mode in the evenings.
   - o Organize your home screen with only essential apps.
5. **Monitor Your Screen Time:**
   - o Track daily screen time and set goals to reduce it.
   - o Identify apps or activities that consume too much time.
6. **Prioritize Real-World Connection:**
   - o Schedule regular in-person activities with friends or family.
   - o Engage in hobbies or physical activities that don't involve screens.
7. **Protect Your Sleep:**
   - o Avoid screens at least an hour before bedtime.
   - o Charge devices outside your bedroom overnight.
8. **Seek Balance:**
   - o Combine online and offline activities to maintain a well-rounded lifestyle.
   - o Reflect regularly on how technology impacts your stress levels and make adjustments as needed.

Technology doesn't have to be a source of stress—it can be a tool for growth and relaxation when used wisely. By recognizing digital stressors, adopting mindful tech habits, and setting clear boundaries, you can reclaim control over your devices and create a healthier, more balanced relationship with technology. Let's continue building your stress-free life in the next chapter!

Chapter 10: The Art of Saying No Without Guilt

Saying "no" can feel uncomfortable, but it's one of the most powerful skills you can cultivate to reduce stress and protect your time and energy. Learning to say no without guilt enables you to focus on what truly matters, set healthy boundaries, and maintain balance in your personal and professional life. This chapter will guide you through the art of saying no effectively and confidently.

Why "No" is a Complete Sentence

Many of us struggle with saying no because we fear disappointing others or being perceived as unkind. However, constantly saying yes to every request can lead to overwhelm, resentment, and burnout.

- **The Power of No:**
  Saying no is not about rejecting others—it's about affirming your priorities and respecting your limits. Every time you say no to something that doesn't align with your goals or values, you create space for things that do.
- **The Cost of Saying Yes:**
  - Time and energy are finite resources. Overcommitting can leave you stretched too thin to focus on your own needs and responsibilities.
  - Saying yes to things you don't want to do can lead to stress, frustration, and a loss of personal integrity.
- **Reframe Your Perspective:**
  - Think of no as a gift: By being honest about your availability, you prevent overpromising and underdelivering.
  - Remember, no is a complete sentence. It doesn't require lengthy explanations or justifications.

Setting Boundaries in Personal and Professional Life

Boundaries are essential for maintaining healthy relationships and reducing stress. They allow you to communicate your needs clearly and protect your time and energy.

- **How to Identify Your Boundaries:**
  - Reflect on past situations where you felt stressed or taken advantage of. What could you have done differently to protect yourself?
  - Consider your non-negotiables: What activities, values, or relationships are most important to you?

- **Personal Boundaries:**
    - Limit time spent on activities that drain you or don't align with your values.
    - Politely decline social invitations that don't fit into your schedule or priorities.
    - Protect your personal time by scheduling regular self-care.
- **Professional Boundaries:**
    - Communicate your workload clearly with colleagues and supervisors.
    - Set specific hours for work and stick to them.
    - Delegate tasks when possible and avoid taking on responsibilities outside your role.

Setting boundaries ensures you're prioritizing your well-being while fostering mutual respect in your relationships.

Communicating Assertively Without Alienating Others

Saying no assertively doesn't have to be confrontational or hurtful. It's about expressing yourself clearly and respectfully.

- **Tips for Saying No Effectively:**
    - **Be Direct:** Keep your response short and to the point. Example: *"Thank you for thinking of me, but I'm not able to commit to this right now."*
    - **Use Positive Language:** Frame your no in a way that acknowledges the other person's request without apologizing unnecessarily. Example: *"I appreciate the opportunity, but I need to focus on other priorities."*
    - **Offer Alternatives (If Appropriate):** Suggest another resource or person who might be able to help. Example: *"I can't take this on, but I think [Name] might be a great fit for this project."*
    - **Stay Firm:** Avoid being swayed by guilt or pressure. Example: *"I understand this is important, but I'm unable to help at this time."*

- **The Role of Tone and Body Language:**
  - Maintain a calm, steady tone of voice.
  - Use open, confident body language, such as making eye contact and avoiding defensive gestures.

Assertive communication strengthens relationships by fostering honesty and clarity.

Exercise: Practice Scenarios for Saying No Effectively

Use the following scenarios to practice saying no confidently and respectfully. Customize the responses to fit your style and needs.

1. **Scenario: A friend asks you to join an event you're not interested in.**
   - Response: *"Thank you for inviting me, but I'll have to pass this time. Let's catch up another day soon."*
2. **Scenario: A colleague asks you to take on extra work when you're already overwhelmed.**
   - Response: *"I wish I could help, but I'm at full capacity right now. I recommend checking with [another colleague] who may have availability."*
3. **Scenario: A family member asks for a favor that conflicts with your plans.**
   - Response: *"I'd love to help, but I have prior commitments. Let me know if there's another time I can assist."*
4. **Scenario: You're asked to donate time to a cause you care about but can't currently commit to.**
   - Response: *"I truly support your mission, but I'm unable to volunteer right now. Please keep me in mind for future opportunities."*
5. **Scenario: A salesperson tries to pressure you into making a purchase.**
   - Response: *"Thank you, but I'm not interested at this time."* (Then walk away or end the call without further engagement.)

Reflection: After practicing these scenarios, note how it felt to say no. Were you able to remain calm and assertive? What worked well, and what could you improve?

Saying no is a skill that takes practice, but the benefits are transformative. By learning to set boundaries and communicate assertively, you'll reduce stress, protect your time, and cultivate relationships built on mutual respect. In the next chapter, we'll explore creative outlets as a tool for stress relief, helping you channel your energy into meaningful and joyful activities. Let's continue building your empowered, stress-free life!

Chapter 11: Harnessing Creativity for Stress Relief

Creativity is a powerful tool for stress relief, offering a way to express emotions, solve problems, and reconnect with joy. Whether it's through writing, drawing, music, or playful exploration, creative outlets can help you channel stress into something productive and meaningful. In this chapter, we'll explore the connection between creativity and emotional well-being, highlight therapeutic outlets, and provide guided prompts to ignite your creativity.

The Connection Between Creativity and Emotional Well-Being

Engaging in creative activities allows your mind to relax and enter a state of flow, where time seems to stand still and stress melts away.

- **How Creativity Reduces Stress:**
  - **Emotional Expression:** Creativity provides a safe space to process and release emotions.
  - **Problem-Solving:** Art and play encourage thinking outside the box, helping you approach challenges with fresh perspectives.
  - **Mindfulness:** Creative activities focus your attention on the present moment, similar to meditation.
- **The Science Behind It:**
  Studies show that engaging in creative activities reduces cortisol levels and increases dopamine, the brain's "feel-good" neurotransmitter. Regular creative expression also boosts resilience and improves overall mental health.

Journaling, Drawing, and Music as Therapeutic Outlets

- **Journaling:**
  Writing allows you to clarify your thoughts, explore your feelings, and reflect on your experiences.
  - **Stream of Consciousness:** Write freely without worrying about grammar or structure. Let your thoughts flow.
  - **Gratitude Journaling:** Focus on the positive by listing three things you're grateful for each day.
  - **Reflective Journaling:** Explore a specific challenge or emotion, and consider what you've learned from it.
- **Drawing and Painting:**
  Visual art taps into the subconscious, offering a non-verbal way to express emotions.
  - **Doodle Your Feelings:** Use shapes, colors, and lines to represent how you feel.

- o **Mandala Coloring:** Filling in intricate designs can be deeply meditative.
- o **Abstract Art:** Paint or draw intuitively, focusing on movement and color rather than creating something realistic.
- **Music:**
  Listening to or creating music can elevate your mood and provide a therapeutic release.
  - o **Play an Instrument:** Experiment with melodies or beats that reflect your emotions.
  - o **Sing or Hum:** Use your voice to connect with the rhythm of your feelings.
  - o **Curate Playlists:** Create playlists that evoke calm, energy, or joy, depending on what you need.

Using Play to Reignite Joy and Reduce Tension

As adults, we often forget the importance of play, but incorporating playful activities can reawaken joy and reduce tension.

- **The Benefits of Play:**
  - o Encourages spontaneity and laughter, which reduce stress hormones.
  - o Improves creativity and problem-solving abilities.
  - o Strengthens social bonds when shared with others.
- **Playful Activities to Try:**
  - o Build something with LEGO or blocks.
  - o Play a board game or solve a puzzle.
  - o Dance freely to your favorite music.
  - o Engage in outdoor activities like frisbee, kite flying, or hiking.

Play doesn't have to be productive—it's about rediscovering the simple pleasures of life.

Activity: Guided Prompts for Creative Expression

1. **Journaling Prompts:**
   - Describe a time you overcame a challenge and what you learned from it.
   - Write about your dream day—what would it look and feel like?
   - List 10 things that bring you joy and how you can incorporate them into your life.
2. **Art Prompts:**
   - Draw or paint an abstract representation of your current mood.
   - Create a vision board using magazine clippings, photos, or sketches.
   - Design a symbol or image that represents your personal resilience.
3. **Music Prompts:**
   - Write lyrics or a poem inspired by your emotions.
   - Experiment with a simple beat or melody on an instrument or app.
   - Create a playlist of songs that evoke calm and listen to it during moments of stress.
4. **Play Prompts:**
   - Try a new activity you haven't done since childhood, like finger painting or hopscotch.
   - Invent a game with your family or friends.
   - Take on a playful challenge, such as building the tallest tower with household items.

Harnessing creativity allows you to transform stress into a source of strength and inspiration. By journaling your thoughts, exploring artistic expression, and embracing the joy of play, you'll cultivate a deeper sense of emotional balance and fulfillment. Let your creativity flow—it's a powerful pathway to a stress-free, empowered life!

Chapter 12: Financial Stress and How to Manage It

Money can be a significant source of stress, affecting every aspect of life, from relationships to mental and physical well-being. However, financial stress doesn't have to control you. By understanding the sources of financial anxiety, adopting practical strategies to manage your finances, and shifting to an abundance mindset, you can regain control and create a more secure and fulfilling relationship with money.

Understanding the Sources of Financial Anxiety

Financial stress often stems from both tangible and psychological factors. Identifying the root causes of your anxiety is the first step to addressing it effectively.

- **Common Sources of Financial Stress:**
  - **Debt:** Ongoing payments, high-interest rates, and mounting balances can feel overwhelming.
  - **Uncertainty:** Irregular income or job instability creates fear about meeting expenses.
  - **Unexpected Expenses:** Medical bills, car repairs, or emergencies can derail your budget.
  - **Lack of Savings:** Feeling unprepared for the future amplifies anxiety.
  - **Comparison:** Social media and peer pressure can create unrealistic expectations about wealth and lifestyle.
- **How Financial Stress Impacts Your Life:**
  - **Mental Health:** Anxiety, depression, and difficulty concentrating.
  - **Physical Health:** Sleep disturbances, high blood pressure, and chronic tension.
  - **Relationships:** Conflicts over money and strained communication.

Acknowledging these sources helps you take proactive steps to manage them.

Budgeting Basics to Regain Control

A well-crafted budget is the cornerstone of financial stability and stress management. It provides a clear picture of your income, expenses, and savings, empowering you to make informed decisions.

- **Steps to Create a Stress-Free Budget:**
  1. **Track Your Spending:** Keep a record of every expense for a month to identify patterns. Use apps like Mint or YNAB (You Need a Budget) for convenience.
  2. **Categorize Expenses:** Divide your spending into essential (e.g., rent, groceries) and non-essential (e.g., dining out, subscriptions) categories.
  3. **Set Limits:** Allocate a specific amount for each category based on your income and priorities.
  4. **Automate Savings:** Direct a portion of your income into a savings account each month, even if it's a small amount.
  5. **Plan for the Unexpected:** Build an emergency fund to cover 3–6 months' worth of essential expenses.
- **Tips for Sticking to Your Budget:**
  o Use cash for discretionary spending to avoid overspending.
  o Regularly review and adjust your budget as needed.
  o Celebrate milestones, like paying off a debt or reaching a savings goal.

Budgeting is not about restriction—it's about aligning your spending with your values and goals.

Cultivating an Abundance Mindset Despite Challenges

An abundance mindset focuses on opportunities rather than limitations, helping you approach financial challenges with optimism and creativity.

- **How to Shift from Scarcity to Abundance:**
  o **Reframe Negative Thoughts:** Replace thoughts like, *"I'll never have enough,"* with, *"I'm taking steps to create financial security."*
  o **Practice Gratitude:** Regularly acknowledge what you have, whether it's a steady income, supportive relationships, or personal strengths.

- o **Focus on Growth:** View financial setbacks as opportunities to learn and adapt.
- **Building Habits to Support Abundance:**
  - o **Invest in Yourself:** Pursue education, skills, or experiences that enhance your earning potential.
  - o **Diversify Income:** Explore side hustles or passive income opportunities.
  - o **Give Back:** Donating time or resources fosters a sense of wealth and generosity.

Cultivating an abundance mindset helps you see money as a tool for achieving your goals, not a source of fear.

Tool: A Financial Stress Assessment and Action Plan

Use this assessment and action plan to evaluate your financial situation and create a path to stability:

1. **Assess Your Financial Stress:**
   - o What are my biggest financial worries?
   - o How often do I feel anxious about money?
   - o How is financial stress affecting my relationships, work, or health?
2. **Evaluate Your Financial Health:**
   - o Total Monthly Income:

     _____

   - o Total Monthly Expenses:

     _____

   - o Debt Balance:

     _____

   - o Savings Balance:

     _____

3. **Set Financial Goals:**
    o Short-Term Goal (1–3 months):
    _____
    o Medium-Term Goal (6–12 months):
    _____
    o Long-Term Goal (1–5 years):
    _____

4. **Create an Action Plan:**
    o **Step 1:** Reduce one non-essential expense this month.
    o **Step 2:** Set up automatic transfers to a savings account.
    o **Step 3:** Choose one debt to focus on paying off using the snowball or avalanche method.
    o **Step 4:** Schedule a monthly check-in to review your progress.

5. **Track Your Progress:**
    o Use a journal, spreadsheet, or financial app to monitor your income, expenses, and savings.
    o Reflect on your achievements and adjust your goals as needed.

Financial stress can feel overwhelming, but with the right tools and mindset, you can regain control and build a secure future. By understanding the sources of your anxiety, creating a realistic budget, and adopting an abundance mindset, you'll transform your relationship with money into one of empowerment and opportunity. Let's continue building your stress-free life in the next chapter!

Chapter 13: Parenting and Stress: Finding the Balance

Parenthood is one of life's most rewarding roles, but it also comes with unique challenges and stresses. Between managing schedules, nurturing relationships, and meeting daily responsibilities, parents often struggle to find balance. This chapter provides strategies for juggling parenthood and self-care, teaching stress management to children, and creating a harmonious family environment that promotes calm and connection.

Juggling Parenthood and Self-Care

As a parent, it's easy to put your needs last. However, prioritizing self-care isn't selfish—it's essential for maintaining your well-being and being the best version of yourself for your children.

- **Why Self-Care Matters:**
    - Replenishes your energy and reduces burnout.
    - Improves patience, focus, and emotional regulation.
    - Sets a healthy example for your children.
- **Practical Self-Care Tips for Busy Parents:**
    - **Schedule "Me Time":** Block out regular time for activities that relax and recharge you, whether it's reading, exercising, or enjoying a hobby.
    - **Delegate and Share Responsibilities:** Ask for help from your partner, family members, or friends when you need a break.
    - **Simplify Your Routine:** Focus on what truly matters and let go of perfectionism. Streamline chores and use tools like meal planning to save time.
    - **Practice Mini Self-Care:** Even 5–10 minutes of deep breathing, stretching, or sipping a cup of tea can make a difference during a busy day.

Teaching Stress Management to Kids

Children are not immune to stress and teaching them healthy coping strategies from a young age helps build resilience and emotional intelligence.

- **Signs Your Child May Be Stressed:**
    - Changes in behavior, such as irritability, withdrawal, or aggression.
    - Physical symptoms, like stomachaches or difficulty sleeping.
    - Avoidance of school or activities they usually enjoy.

- **Stress Management Techniques for Kids:**
  - **Deep Breathing:** Teach your child to take slow, deep breaths by pretending to blow up a balloon or imagining a flower they're smelling.
  - **Name the Feeling:** Encourage them to label their emotions, such as "I feel sad" or "I feel nervous." Naming emotions helps them feel less overwhelming.
  - **Create a Calm Space:** Designate a quiet corner with comforting items like books, stuffed animals, or coloring supplies where your child can retreat to when feeling stressed.
  - **Problem-Solving:** Help them break big problems into smaller steps and brainstorm solutions together.
- **Modeling Healthy Coping:**
  - Show your child how you manage stress by staying calm, practicing gratitude, and discussing your emotions openly.

Creating a Calm Family Environment

A peaceful home environment helps reduce stress for everyone and fosters stronger relationships.

- **Establish Family Routines:**
  - Predictable routines provide stability and help children feel secure. Create morning, mealtime, and bedtime routines that work for everyone.
- **Encourage Open Communication:**
  - Make time for regular family check-ins where everyone can share their thoughts, feelings, and concerns without judgment.
- **Reduce Clutter:**
  - A clutter-free home creates a sense of calm. Involve the whole family in organizing and tidying shared spaces.

- **Foster Positive Interactions:**
  - Use positive reinforcement and praise to encourage good behavior. Focus on the good rather than criticizing the bad.
- **Limit Screen Time:**
  - Too much screen time can contribute to stress and disrupt sleep. Set boundaries for device use and encourage screen-free family activities.

By fostering a calm, supportive environment, you create a safe space for everyone to thrive.

Activity: Stress-Reducing Activities for Parents and Children

Here are some fun and effective activities that both parents and children can enjoy to relieve stress together:

1. **Mindful Movement:**
   - Practice simple yoga poses, such as Tree Pose or Cat-Cow, with your child.
   - Play a game of "freeze dance," where everyone stops and takes a deep breath when the music pauses.
2. **Creative Expression:**
   - Draw or paint your "happy place" as a family, and share what makes it special.
   - Create a "gratitude tree" by writing things you're thankful for on leaves and attaching them to a paper tree.
3. **Outdoor Adventures:**
   - Take a walk in nature and play a "scavenger hunt" game, looking for specific items like a bird, a flower, or a unique rock.
   - Plant a small garden or care for potted plants together.
4. **Storytime with a Twist:**
   - Read a calming book together, such as one with positive messages or relaxation themes.

- o Create your own bedtime story, letting each family member add to the tale.
5. **Breathing Games:**
   - o Blow bubbles and focus on slow, steady breaths to make the biggest bubbles.
   - o Pretend to blow out candles, practicing long, controlled exhales.
6. **Family Gratitude Jar:**
   - o Each night, write down one thing you're grateful for on a slip of paper and add it to the jar. At the end of the week, read them together.

Parenting is challenging, but it doesn't have to be overwhelming. By prioritizing self-care, teaching your children healthy coping skills, and fostering a calm family environment, you can create a balanced and fulfilling life for your family. In the next chapter, we'll explore cultural perspectives on stress management, offering insights and practices from around the world. Let's continue this journey to a stress-free life together!

Chapter 14: Cultural Perspectives on Stress Management

Stress is a universal experience, but the ways people cope with it vary widely across cultures. From ancient traditions to modern practices, different societies have developed unique approaches to managing stress that reflect their values and lifestyles. In this chapter, we'll explore stress reduction practices from around the world, learn how to incorporate global wisdom into our own lives, and uncover valuable lessons from cultures with lower stress levels.

Stress Reduction Practices Around the World

Each culture has its own time-tested methods for managing stress. These practices often integrate physical, mental, and spiritual well-being, offering holistic approaches to relaxation and resilience.

- **Japan: Shinrin-Yoku (Forest Bathing):**
  Immersing oneself in nature is a cornerstone of Japanese stress relief. Forest bathing involves walking slowly and mindfully in a natural setting, allowing the sights, sounds, and smells to soothe the mind and body.
- **India: Ayurveda:**
  This ancient system of medicine emphasizes balance among the body, mind, and spirit. Practices like yoga, meditation, and dietary adjustments tailored to one's dosha (body type) are central to stress management in Ayurveda.
- **China: Tai Chi and Qigong:**
  These gentle martial arts combine slow, flowing movements with deep breathing and focused awareness. They promote physical health, mental clarity, and emotional balance.
- **Sweden: Fika (Coffee Breaks):**
  In Sweden, fika is more than a coffee break—it's a cultural ritual. Taking time to slow down, enjoy a hot beverage, and connect with others fosters relaxation and community.
- **Hawaii: Ho'oponopono:**
  This traditional Hawaiian practice focuses on forgiveness and reconciliation. By repeating phrases like, "I'm sorry, please forgive me, thank you, I love you," individuals can release stress and heal emotional wounds.
- **Italy: Dolce Far Niente (The Sweetness of Doing Nothing):**
  Italians celebrate the art of slowing down and savoring life's simple pleasures. Whether it's a leisurely meal or a stroll through a piazza, this mindset prioritizes relaxation over busyness.

Incorporating Global Wisdom: Ayurveda, Tai Chi, and More

You don't need to travel the world to benefit from these practices. Many can be adapted to fit into your daily life:

- **Try Forest Bathing:**
  Spend time in a park or natural setting, focusing on your surroundings without distractions. Even 15–20 minutes can reduce stress.
- **Practice Yoga or Tai Chi:**
  Look for beginner classes online or in your community to experience the physical and mental benefits of these ancient practices.
- **Adopt a Mindful Eating Habit:**
  Take a page from Italy's dolce far niente and savor your meals without multitasking. Engage your senses and appreciate each bite.
- **Engage in Gratitude Rituals:**
  Inspired by Ho'oponopono, create a daily gratitude practice that focuses on forgiveness and appreciation.
- **Incorporate Relaxing Rituals:**
  Create your version of fika by setting aside time each day to enjoy tea or coffee mindfully and connect with loved ones.

By blending these practices into your routine, you can infuse your life with calm and intention.

What We Can Learn from Cultures with Lower Stress Levels

Some cultures consistently report lower stress levels and higher life satisfaction. Here's what we can learn from their lifestyles:

- **Community Connection:**
  Cultures like those in Denmark and Costa Rica emphasize the importance of strong social ties. Sharing meals, spending time with family, and participating in community activities build support networks that buffer against stress.

- **Work-Life Balance:**
  Scandinavian countries prioritize work-life balance through policies like shorter workweeks and extended parental leave. Protecting personal time allows for greater relaxation and fulfillment.
- **Respect for Rest and Play:**
  In cultures like Italy and Spain, midday breaks (siestas) and unhurried meals are cultural norms. These practices remind us to slow down and recharge.
- **Living in Harmony with Nature:**
  Indigenous communities and rural cultures often have a deep connection to nature, which fosters mindfulness and reduces anxiety. Spending time outdoors helps regulate stress hormones and improves mood.
- **Minimalism and Simplicity:**
  Cultures that value simplicity, like Japan and Bhutan, often experience less stress because they focus on what truly matters—relationships, purpose, and well-being—rather than material possessions.

Insight: A Comparison of Stress Management Strategies Across Cultures

Culture	Practice	Key Benefit
Japan	Shinrin-Yoku (Forest Bathing)	Reduces cortisol, promotes mindfulness
India	Ayurveda	Balances mind, body, and spirit
China	Tai Chi/Qigong	Enhances physical and mental harmony
Sweden	Fika	Encourages relaxation and social connection
Hawaii	Ho'oponopono	Heals emotional wounds and fosters forgiveness
Italy	Dolce Far Niente	Celebrates slowing down and savoring life

Stress is universal, but so are the solutions. By incorporating global wisdom into your daily routine, you can benefit from the collective knowledge of diverse cultures. Whether it's practicing mindfulness, embracing simplicity, or fostering connection, these practices remind us that managing stress is not just about survival—it's about thriving. In the next chapter, we'll explore strategies for crisis stress management, equipping you to handle life's most challenging moments with resilience and grace. Let's continue this empowering journey!

Chapter 15: Crisis Stress Management

Life is full of unexpected events, and some of them can be profoundly challenging. Major crises, such as the loss of a loved one, divorce, or a career setback, can test your emotional resilience and ability to cope. This chapter focuses on strategies to manage stress during life's most difficult moments, offering guidance on building a crisis-response plan and knowing when to seek professional help.

Coping During Major Life Events

Crises can disrupt your sense of stability, leaving you feeling overwhelmed and vulnerable. Understanding how to navigate these moments is essential for maintaining your emotional well-being.

- **Common Major Life Events and Their Impacts:**
  - **Loss of a Loved One:** Grief can trigger a wide range of emotions, from sadness and anger to guilt and numbness. It's important to allow yourself to feel and process these emotions.
  - **Divorce or Relationship Breakups:** These events often involve a mix of grief, relief, and uncertainty. They may also affect your financial and social life.
  - **Career Changes or Job Loss:** Losing a job can lead to feelings of inadequacy, fear about the future, and financial stress.
- **Tips for Coping During Major Crises:**
  - **Acknowledge Your Feelings:** Allow yourself to feel without judgment. Bottling up emotions can lead to greater stress.
  - **Lean on Your Support System:** Share your thoughts and feelings with trusted friends, family, or support groups.
  - **Focus on What You Can Control:** Identify small, actionable steps to regain a sense of stability and purpose.
  - **Practice Self-Compassion:** Remind yourself that it's okay to struggle and that healing takes time.

Building a Crisis-Response Plan

Having a plan in place for handling crises can help you respond more effectively and reduce the chaos during stressful times.

- **Steps to Create a Crisis-Response Plan:**
  1. **Identify Potential Stressors:** Think about life events that could disrupt your stability (e.g., financial troubles, health issues, or relationship challenges).
  2. **Develop a Support Network:** Know who you can turn to for emotional, practical, or professional support.
  3. **Create a Financial Safety Net:** Build an emergency fund to cover unexpected expenses during tough times.
  4. **Prepare a Resource List:** Keep a list of helpful contacts, such as therapists, financial advisors, or legal professionals.
  5. **Practice Stress-Relief Techniques:** Regularly engage in activities that help you stay calm, such as meditation, exercise, or journaling.
- **What to Do in the Heat of a Crisis:**
  - Take a moment to breathe deeply and calm your nervous system.
  - Break down the situation into manageable pieces. Focus on one issue at a time.
  - Reach out for support. Isolation can amplify stress.

Having a plan doesn't eliminate the challenges of a crisis, but it equips you with tools to face them more confidently.

Finding Professional Help When You Need It

Sometimes, the weight of a crisis requires outside assistance. Knowing when and how to seek professional help is a vital part of managing stress effectively.

- **When to Seek Professional Help:**
  - You feel unable to function in your daily life.
  - Your physical or mental health is deteriorating.
  - You experience persistent feelings of hopelessness or despair.

- o Relationships with loved ones are significantly strained.
- **Types of Professionals to Consider:**
  - o **Therapists or Counselors:** Provide emotional support and coping strategies.
  - o **Financial Advisors:** Help navigate financial challenges or plan for recovery.
  - o **Legal Professionals:** Assist with matters such as divorce or estate planning.
  - o **Crisis Hotlines:** Offer immediate support for those in emotional distress.
- **How to Find the Right Help:**
  - o Ask for recommendations from trusted sources.
  - o Research providers to find one that aligns with your needs and values.
  - o Don't hesitate to try different options until you find the right fit.

Seeking help is a sign of strength, not weakness. It shows that you're taking proactive steps to regain control.

Checklist: Steps to Take in a Personal or Professional Crisis

Use this checklist as a guide when facing a crisis:

1. **Pause and Breathe:**
   - o Take a few deep breaths to center yourself and reduce immediate stress.
2. **Assess the Situation:**
   - o What is the primary issue you're facing?
   - o Are there any immediate dangers or urgent actions needed?
3. **Reach Out for Support:**
   - o Who in your support network can help?
   - o Do you need professional assistance?

4. **Break Down the Problem:**
   - o Divide the crisis into smaller, manageable tasks.
   - o Focus on what you can control in the moment.
5. **Create an Action Plan:**
   - o Identify the next steps you need to take.
   - o Set realistic goals and prioritize tasks.
6. **Practice Self-Care:**
   - o Engage in activities that calm and ground you, such as exercise, journaling, or meditation.
   - o Ensure you're getting enough rest, nutrition, and hydration.
7. **Reflect and Adjust:**
   - o Review your progress regularly.
   - o Be flexible and adapt your approach as the situation evolves.

Crises are a natural part of life, but they don't have to define you. By developing coping strategies, building a crisis-response plan, and seeking help when needed, you can navigate even the most challenging situations with resilience and grace. In the next chapter, we'll bring everything together to help you master long-term stress management and maintain balance in all areas of your life. Let's continue on this empowering journey!

Conclusion: Becoming the Master of Your Inner World

Mastering stress isn't about eliminating it entirely—it's about transforming your relationship with it. Stress is a natural part of life, a sign that you're engaged, striving, and connected to the world around you. The goal is not to avoid stress but to navigate life's inevitable challenges with grace, confidence, and resilience.

This journey is about reclaiming control over your inner world. By applying the tools and strategies in this book, you've begun the process of transforming stress from a source of overwhelm into an opportunity for growth and empowerment.

Reflecting on the Journey

Think back to where you started. Perhaps you were feeling stretched too thin, struggling to juggle responsibilities, or unsure how to handle mounting pressures. As you've progressed through these chapters, you've gained insight into the nature of stress, developed actionable strategies, and cultivated a deeper understanding of your own needs and strengths.

Let's recap the pillars of stress mastery you've built along the way:

1. **Understanding Stress:** You've learned to identify stressors and break the stress cycle with awareness and intention.
2. **Mindset Transformation:** By embracing positive thinking, self-compassion, and a proactive mindset, you've shifted how you respond to challenges.
3. **Time and Boundaries:** Through prioritization, saying no, and creating balance, you've taken control of your time and energy.
4. **Breathing and Relaxation:** Breathing techniques, mindfulness, and relaxation practices have become your tools for instant calm.
5. **Physical and Emotional Strategies:** Exercise, nutrition, emotional resilience, and creative outlets have strengthened your body and mind.
6. **Leveraging Support:** You've learned the value of community, connection, and seeking help when needed.
7. **Adopting a Global Perspective:** You've drawn wisdom from diverse cultures, enriching your approach to stress management.
8. **Crisis Mastery:** By preparing for life's major challenges, you've equipped yourself with tools to handle even the toughest moments.

These practices are more than just techniques—they are habits and mindsets that will serve you for a lifetime.

The Power of Choice

At the heart of stress mastery is the understanding that you have a choice. While you can't always control external circumstances, you can control how you respond to them. Every day, you have the opportunity to choose how you allocate your time, energy, and focus.

- **Choose Presence:** Be fully engaged in the moment rather than worrying about the past or future.
- **Choose Growth:** View challenges as opportunities to learn and improve.
- **Choose Self-Care:** Prioritize your well-being so you can show up as your best self for others.
- **Choose Gratitude:** Focus on the positive aspects of your life, even during tough times.

Empowerment begins with these choices. When you recognize your agency, you unlock the ability to create a life of balance, resilience, and fulfillment.

Looking Ahead

Mastering stress is not a destination—it's a lifelong practice. As life evolves, new challenges will arise, but so will new opportunities for growth. The tools you've gained here will help you adapt, no matter what the future holds.

- **Stay Committed to Growth:** Continue learning, experimenting, and refining your strategies. What works now may evolve as your life changes.
- **Celebrate Your Progress:** Acknowledge the victories, big and small, that you achieve along the way.
- **Be Kind to Yourself:** Perfection is not the goal. Embrace the journey, including its setbacks, as part of your growth.

Your Invitation to Thrive

Stress will always be part of the human experience, but it doesn't have to define your life. You now have the knowledge, tools, and confidence to turn stress into a stepping stone rather than a stumbling block.

Imagine a life where you wake up feeling calm and centered, knowing you have the resources to handle whatever comes your way. Picture yourself navigating challenges with resilience, maintaining balance in your relationships, career, and personal growth. This is not just a possibility—it's a reality you're capable of creating.

This book has laid the foundation, but the next step is yours to take. Integrate these strategies into your daily life, share what you've learned with others, and continue building a life that reflects your values, passions, and potential.

Final Thought

Your inner world is yours to master. By taking control of your thoughts, emotions, and actions, you empower yourself to thrive—not in spite of stress, but because of how you've learned to embrace and navigate it. The journey to a balanced, empowered life begins and ends with you.

You are capable. You are resilient. You are the master of your inner world.

Now, go forth and thrive.

Bonus Content

This bonus section offers practical tools and resources to support your ongoing stress management journey. Whether you need a quick reference guide, recommendations for apps and tools, or access to online support, these resources will empower you to stay calm, focused, and resilient.

Quick Reference Cheat Sheet for Managing Stress

When You're Feeling Overwhelmed:

- **Pause and Breathe:** Try box breathing (inhale for 4 counts, hold for 4 counts, exhale for 4 counts, and hold again for 4 counts).
- **Reframe Your Thoughts:** Ask yourself, *"What's within my control?"* and focus on actionable steps.
- **Take a Break:** Step away from the stressor for 5–10 minutes to clear your mind.

Daily Practices to Reduce Stress:

- **Morning Rituals:** Start your day with gratitude journaling or light stretching.
- **Move Your Body:** Exercise for at least 20–30 minutes daily, even if it's a walk.
- **Mindful Moments:** Practice mindfulness by focusing on the present moment during routine activities.
- **Connect with Others:** Spend time with friends or loved ones to boost your mood.

Stress-Relieving Activities:

- Take a nature walk or practice forest bathing.
- Engage in creative outlets like drawing, journaling, or playing music.
- Unplug from screens and enjoy a tech-free hour.

Affirmations for Calm and Confidence:

- *"I am in control of my thoughts and actions."*
- *"I have the strength to face any challenge."*
- *"Each breath I take brings me closer to calm."*

Recommended Apps and Tools for Stress Management

Meditation and Mindfulness Apps:

1. **Calm:** Guided meditations, sleep stories, and relaxation exercises for stress relief.
   - Download Calm
2. **Headspace:** Offers beginner-friendly meditations and mindfulness programs.
   - Download Headspace
3. **Insight Timer:** Free meditations and courses tailored to various stress management needs.
   - Download Insight Timer

Productivity and Focus Apps:

1. **Forest:** Helps you stay focused by growing virtual trees when you avoid distractions.
   - Download Forest
2. **Todoist:** Organize tasks and reduce mental clutter with this simple to-do list app.
   - Download Todoist
3. **RescueTime:** Tracks screen time to help you identify and reduce digital distractions.
   - Download RescueTime

Fitness and Relaxation Apps:

1. **Yoga for Beginners:** Easy-to-follow yoga routines for stress relief and flexibility.
   - Available on iOS and Android.
2. **FitOn:** Free workout videos, including yoga, Pilates, and stretching for relaxation.
   - Download FitOn
3. **White Noise:** Soothing sounds to improve sleep and create a calming atmosphere.
   - Available on iOS and Android.

Exclusive Access to Online Resources and Support Groups

Online Resources for Stress Management:

1. **UCLA Mindful Awareness Research Center:** Free mindfulness meditations and resources.
   - Visit UCLA Mindfulness
2. **American Institute of Stress:** Articles, tools, and strategies for managing stress.
   - Visit AIS
3. **Positive Psychology:** A collection of science-backed tools and techniques for mental well-being.
   - Visit Positive Psychology

Support Groups and Communities:

1. **Daily Strength:** Online forums for sharing experiences and advice on stress and anxiety.
   - Join Daily Strength
2. **BetterHelp:** Access to licensed therapists for online counseling and support.
   - Visit BetterHelp
3. **Reddit Stress Communities:** Subreddits like r/Stress and r/Anxiety offer peer support and tips.
   - Explore Reddit

Exclusive Community Access:
Sign up for our exclusive online support group, where readers of this book can connect, share experiences, and participate in live stress management workshops.

- Join Our Community (Link placeholder—customize for your community or website)

Your Next Steps

Stress management is a lifelong journey, and having the right tools and support makes all the difference. Use these resources to reinforce what you've learned, explore new strategies, and connect with others who share your goals. You have everything you need to thrive—now it's time to take action and create a life of calm, confidence, and resilience!

Acknowledgments

This book would not have been possible without the unwavering support and encouragement of so many incredible individuals. I extend my deepest gratitude to my family, friends, and mentors, whose belief in me has been a constant source of inspiration. Your guidance and love have fueled my determination and passion every step of the way.

To the readers who have chosen to embark on this journey, thank you for trusting me to be a part of your path to success. Your dreams are the driving force behind my mission, and it is my deepest hope that this book empowers you to unlock your true potential and sell beyond limits.

Copyright Notice

Disclaimer

Breaking The Stress Code "Master the Art of Calm & Control"

is a copyrighted work of non-fiction. Names, characters, businesses, organizations, places, events, and incidents mentioned in this publication are either the product of the author's imagination or used fictitiously. Any resemblance to actual persons, living or deceased, events, or locales is purely coincidental.

This book is for informational and educational purposes only. It does not constitute financial, investment, or legal advice. Readers are encouraged to do their own research (DYOR) and consult with professionals before making any financial or investment decisions. The author and publisher are not liable for any outcomes resulting from actions taken based on the content of this book.